World's Worst Cars

Craig Cheetham

ROSEN
PUBLISHING®

New York

This edition first published in 2009 by:

The Rosen Publishing Group, Inc.
29 E. 21st Street
New York, NY 10010

Project Editor: Michael Spilling
Picture Research: James Hollingworth
Design: Hawes Media

On the cover: the British Bond Bug, which was made
from 1970-1974.

Library of Congress Cataloging-in-Publication Data

Cheetham, Craig.
World's worst cars / Craig Cheetham.—1st ed.
    p. cm.—(World's worst—from innovation to disaster)
Includes bibliographical references and index.
ISBN-13: 978-1-4042-1844-4 (lib. binding)
1. Automobiles—Design and construction—History.
2. Automobiles—Defects—History. I. Title.
TL240.C3787 2009
629.222—dc22

                                    2008016080

Manufactured in the United States of America

CONTENTS

INTRODUCTION

There are hundreds of books about the world's best cars. Some models even have entire volumes dedicated to them. But what about the auto industry's underclass? The cars that spent their lives as the butts of many a joke, suffered at the hands of stand-up comedians and earned their place in the annals of motoring history not for what they achieved, but for what they didn't. Despite their many and various faults, some of them even made a dedicated band of owners very happy.

This book is dedicated to the underdogs: the design disasters, financial failures, and motoring misfits that make the auto industry such a fascinating and exciting field in which to work. It is in no way intended to insult and deride these machines. After all, a car may have become a spectacular failure after its launch, but you can be sure that, somewhere along the line, it was the dream of at least one person. The world also needs brilliant engineers, and those in the motor industry are, and always have been, among the global elite. This book intends not to slight their achievements, but to go some way to explaining why some of the world's least spectacular cars came into being.

Each of the models has been chosen for a particular reason, and the opinions expressed are my own. There are many more cars out there that could easily qualify for selection, and you may feel that some of the cars

Above: *Leyland Australia marketed the P76 as "Anything but average." In reality, it wasn't even good enough to earn "average" status.*

4

Above: *AMC's Eagle may have set the precedent for the current trend toward car-based sports utility vehicles (SUVs), but it was an absolute horror to drive.*

appearing here do not deserve such criticism. Certainly, some of my choices are controversial, but I hope I explain myself fully in the accompanying text. There are even cars in here that I would happily jump to defend. I've owned at least a dozen of the cars in this book, and speak from experience when I say that my memory of owning them was nowhere near as bad as some of the reports they received when new.

I've also tried to make this book as global as possible. Sheer volume means that the majority of cars chosen are from the world's biggest car markets around the world. They are represented here by their own transports of non-delight.

Above all, I want this book to be a tribute to and celebration of the diversity of the motor industry. A car may receive bad press when new, but it can still attract followers; without enthusiasts flying the flag for even the most awful cars ever made, the world would be a much duller place. To those souls brave enough to own, love, and cherish one of the Worst Cars in the World I salute your bravery and originality, and, inevitably, your sense of humor. Take a look at my driveway and you'll see I'm right there with you.

The cars in this title have been split into four categories: Badly Built, Design Disasters, Financial Failures, and Misplaced Marques. A full explanation of the category is provided on the opening page of each section, but it's important to point out that in some cases the cars themselves were less to blame than the marketing departments.

ADVANCE SPECIFICATION | **AUSTIN** 3-LITRE

BADLY BUILT

Not all of the worst cars in the world were born bad. Some were brilliantly conceived and cleverly designed. In many cases, they could have been, and should have been, brilliant, but were let down by the very people that built them. Some of them, including the Alfa Romeo Alfasud and Rover SD1, were brilliantly received on their debuts. The press hailed their design supremacy and, only later, after serious faults started to manifest themselves, did it become apparent that their owners were in for sleepless nights and financial hardship.

Others, of course, were complete duds from the outset. Cars such as the Austin Allegro and Renault 14 were not that desirable to start off with—and then shocking reliability records destroyed their last vestiges of respectability. Over the next few pages, we have detailed the absolute low points of the global motor industry. Not only were these cars some of the worst ever built, but also they were not even built properly to start with . . .

Left: *British Leyland's stillborn Austin 3-Litre was one of the most dreadful cars of its era, in every conceivable respect.*

ASTON MARTIN LAGONDA *(1975–90)*

Aston Martin already knew how to create cars that turned heads, but the Lagonda was something new and different from the company famous for its elegant but reserved styling. In true 1970s fashion, the four-door luxury sedan was wedge-shaped. And what a wedge it was! From bow to stern, the Lagonda was a dramatic if rather vulgar piece of styling, while inside it bristled with new electronic technology, including an all-LCD instrument pack. But sadly, it was underdeveloped, and electrical problems were rife.

The car's instrument packs gave up, the pop-up headlights stopped popping up and, to make matters worse, the floorpans tended to rot with surprising alacrity for what was such an expensive and flamboyant machine. Today, the Lagonda remains largely snubbed by Aston Martin fans, who much prefer the company's more traditional models.

SPECIFICATIONS

TOP SPEED:	143mph (231km/h)
0–60MPH (0–96KM/H):	8.8secs
ENGINE TYPE:	V8
DISPLACEMENT:	326ci (5340cc)
WEIGHT:	4410lb (1984kg)
MILEAGE:	14mpg
	(20.1l/100km)

Left: *Not even the "New for 1985" walnut dashboard, pepperpot alloy wheels and wood trim were enough to tempt more buyers into William Towns's controversial "Wedge."*

Aston Martin may have claimed that the Lagonda was bristling with new technology, but this did not extend under the hood. The wedge-shaped sedan came with the company's trademark 323ci (5.3-liter) V8 as standard.

The Lagonda's digital LCD dashboard was billed as a technological breakthrough when it first appeared, and other manufacturers did follow suit, but the British company's pioneering attempt at digital instruments was doomed to failure because the units broke down regularly.

Traditional Aston Martin fans did not take to the Lagonda's dramatic styling. It was certainly avant-garde, but few would call it genuinely stylish. It was too long and narrow, and the tail sat too high for the low nose.

It might have been expensive, but the Lagonda still had a build quality that was symptomatic of British models in the 1970s: corrosion was rife, especially in the sills and floor panels.

AUSTIN MAESTRO *(1982–95)*

Oh, dear! With the Allegro and Maxi finally put out to pasture, Austin-Rover was hoping for great things with the Maestro. But it wasn't to be. Once again, the stylists completely misjudged buyers' tastes, and the Maestro's tall stance and large glass areas quickly earned it the unfortunate nickname of "Popemobile" from the British press. Nor did things get any better as the car aged: there were terrible rust problems around the Maestro's rear wheel arches and a dated engine range offered little in the way of performance or refinement.

Top Vanden Plas models came with a speech synthesizer in the dashboard, voiced by New Zealand actress Nicolette Mackenzie. This feature frequently warned of low oil pressure and a lack of fuel, even when the car was in good health, while it barked at you to put your seatbelt on before you even sat down.

SPECIFICATIONS

TOP SPEED:	96mph (155km/h)
0–60MPH (0–96KM/H):	12.3secs
ENGINE TYPE:	in-line four
DISPLACEMENT:	78ci (1275cc)
WEIGHT:	1929lb (868kg)
MILEAGE:	35mpg (8.1l/100km)

Left: The Miracle Maestro—Driving is Believing. Until you've had a spell behind the wheel, it's hard to believe how bad the Maestro actually is . . .

Styling wasn't the Maestro's strong point; its scalloped sides and bulbous rear end sat awkwardly with the excessive glass area, and sleeker rivals made the car look dated at launch. Regardless, it was to remain in production for 12 years.

You could choose from either the awful R-Series 98ci (1.6-liter) engine, the dated 79ci (1.3-liter) A-Series or a distinctly agricultural-sounding diesel. None was great, but at least the gearbox was fairly pleasant. It was borrowed from the Volkswagen Golf.

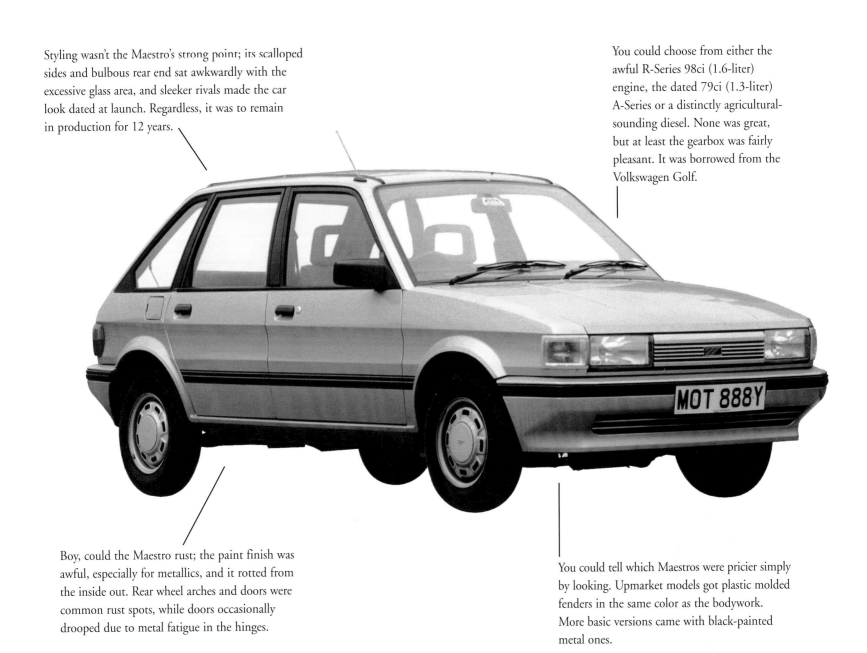

Boy, could the Maestro rust; the paint finish was awful, especially for metallics, and it rotted from the inside out. Rear wheel arches and doors were common rust spots, while doors occasionally drooped due to metal fatigue in the hinges.

You could tell which Maestros were pricier simply by looking. Upmarket models got plastic molded fenders in the same color as the bodywork. More basic versions came with black-painted metal ones.

CHEVROLET NOVA (1970–79)

The Nova could have been, and should have been, a very good car. Its styling was in keeping with the tastes of its era, and the design was spacious and reasonably economical. But it was General Motors' cost-cutting that caused damage to the model's reputation. Built as an entry-level six-cylinder model for families on a budget, it was sparsely equipped, while the cabin was trimmed in wall-to-wall black plastic. Spending time inside one was like spending time in purgatory thanks to brittle plastics that snapped easily, while excessive oil consumption and rust around the rear wheel arches did nothing to enhance the model's reputation.

Owners also reported regular gearbox faults and cylinder head problems, while some models suffered from inexplicably rotten floorpans. The SS396 V8-engine sports model, on the other hand, was really quite interesting . . .

SPECIFICATIONS	
TOP SPEED:	95mph (153km/h)
0–60MPH (0–96KM/H):	16.4secs
ENGINE TYPE:	in-line four
DISPLACEMENT:	139ci (2286cc)
WEIGHT:	2246lb (1010kg)
MILEAGE:	24mpg
	(11.8l/100km)

Left: *If you were prepared to "take it to the limit," you needed nerves of steel. Despite the advertising campaign, the Nova was not a focused driver's car.*

It looked okay from the outside, but once you climbed inside a Nova, you knew you were in a cheap car. The plastics were shiny and brittle, while the black PVC seats got so hot that they burned bare skin in sunny weather.

Oddly, the Nova was fairly rust-resistant around its front end, but the rear used to rot with alarming speed. It made the car look like it was in fact two different models welded together, as the front was usually in far better condition!

The Nova was very much a non-entity in the handling department. There were cars that cornered better than it did, but it wasn't as bad as many softly sprung and unpredictable American sedans of the 1970s. At least, not until the suspension bushes wore out, which they often did.

With six cylinders and reasonable fuel economy, the Nova's engine looked attractive to buyers who were on a budget. But while it was fairly thrifty at the pumps, it guzzled oil like it was going out of fashion.

DATSUN 120Y *(1974–78)*

The 120Y—also known as "Sunny"—put Japan's fledgling car industry firmly on the map, racking up an astonishing number of sales: 2.4 million across Europe and America in a four-year production run. It did this by offering value for money and generous specification levels. Despite the model's early promise, owners discovered in later years that the car was far less good a package than they first thought.

While the cars were mechanically almost unbreakable, it soon became apparent that the Japanese weren't very good at rust-proofing, and the 120Y acquired a reputation on the secondhand market as something of a terrible car, with rust eating its way into the sills, trunk floors, firewalls, and subframes faster than a plague of woodworm in a lumber yard.

SPECIFICATIONS

TOP SPEED:	90mph (145km/h)
0–60MPH (0–96KM/H):	16.0secs
ENGINE TYPE:	in-line four
DISPLACEMENT:	71ci (1171cc)
WEIGHT:	1757lb (791kg)
MILEAGE:	34mpg (8.3l/100km)

Left: The 120Y was a fairly successful rally car, but its poor handling could surprise even the most skilled of drivers on poor surfaces.

It looked attractive in the brochure. The Datsun had a radio, a heater, reclining seats and a heated rear window as standard—but, though good value, it felt cheap and was poorly finished.

Rot wasn't restricted to the underneath of the vehicle, and many 120Ys started to look shabby very early on. The front panel used to rot so badly that the headlights would sometimes come loose and fall out.

The Datsun's structure was simple, with leaf springs at the rear and independent front suspension. It made for predictable handling on dry roads, but it could be uncomfortably twitchy in the rain.

Structural problems didn't take long to make their presence felt, and the sills, floorpans, and rear subframes were often the first parts of a 120Y to see the business end of a welding gun.

FORD MAVERICK *(1969–73)*

Yet another car that seemed fine when it was new, but which turned out to be a badly built disaster on wheels, the Ford Maverick lost its reputation to metal fatigue. There were four-door and two-door models, as well as a Mercury version called the Comet. Most were finished in lurid colors with vinyl roofs, and what they all had in common was that they were built on a platform that was heavily prone to rusting.

Nor was their case helped by gutless and fragile in-line six engines. But the cars were cheap and therefore popular, especially during the 1970s fuel crises. While the perilous handling and poor performance were accepted by buyers in the first place, the rot that manifested itself later most certainly wasn't . . .

SPECIFICATIONS

TOP SPEED:	100mph (162km/h)
0–60MPH (0–96KM/H):	15.4secs
ENGINE TYPE:	in-line six
DISPLACEMENT:	170ci (2784cc)
WEIGHT:	2411lb (1084kg)
MILEAGE:	22mpg (12.8l/100km)

Left: *The Maverick had many problems, the biggest being that, whichever angle you viewed it from, it was desperately ugly.*

It was spacious and comfortable, but the Maverick offered few creature comforts. The cabin was normally trimmed in cheap-looking black vinyl, which got unbearably hot during summer months.

Not even the styling could save the Maverick. It wasn't especially offensive, but it was considered rather bland, while two-door versions had far too much metal in the rear quarter panel—a problem, given how rust-prone the metal was.

Ford dropped a blooper with the original Maverick. The floorpan had so many dirt and water traps that it was inevitable rust would eventually take hold, particularly as the cars left the factory with hardly any undersealent.

The car's soft ride and cart-sprung suspension meant handling wasn't the Maverick's forte, while the steering was bad, especially when the steering components started to wear out, causing the mechanism to seize.

LOTUS ELITE/ECLAT (1974–91)

Lotus thought it was being avant-garde when it unveiled the wedge-shaped Elite and Eclat models in 1974, but in reality it produced a pair of plastic-bodied monstrosities, which embodied all that was gaudy and uncultured about 1970s fashion. Perhaps the cars' only saving grace was their gutsy and responsive 2.2-liter engines, but a lack of development soon put an end to this, with coolant leaks causing them to overheat and warp their head gaskets. Electrical faults were even more common, usually caused by rusty earth terminals. It's common to see them driving around with one pop-up headlight popped up, and the other one "sleeping," as a lack of lubrication in the mechanism caused the electric motors inside to burn out. Ironically, as the cheapest entry into Lotus ownership, they have since acquired quite a cult following.

SPECIFICATIONS

TOP SPEED:	124mph (200km/h)
0–60MPH (0–96KM/H):	7.8secs
ENGINE TYPE:	in-line four
DISPLACEMENT:	120ci (1973cc)
WEIGHT:	2503lb (1126kg)
MILEAGE:	28mpg (10l/100km)

Left: *A breath of fresh air from Lotus—or a sharp intake of breath from your local mechanic when he sees that the cylinder head has warped . . .*

The small Lotuses were nothing if not distinctive, and this was evident once you opened the door. As well as having unusually styled seats, the cars had an entire dashboard covered in suede. Most of the switches came from Ford or British Leyland.

Wedge-shaped styling was all the rage in the 1970s, but both the Elite and Eclat looked dated when they first appeared, and the striking profile was so individual to the model that they never improved with age. Also, the fiberglass panels were prone to breaking.

Lotus designed an entirely new 16-valve engine for the Elite and Eclat series—but it wasn't the most reliable unit, especially in early cars. It would overheat, causing the cylinder heads to warp, while head gasket failure was also a regular (and expensive) occurrence.

Bearing in mind that Lotus cut so many corners with the basic design of the Elite and Eclat, it's surprising to find that under the skin is a highly complex, steel backbone chassis, with the fiberglass shell designed specifically to provide some of the car's structural integrity.

DESIGN DISASTERS

Some cars are so dreadful they should never have made it past the initial design stage. But desperate times call for desperate measures, and that means some truly awful machinery has slipped through the net when car makers have realized their project is so far advanced that they can't afford to go back to the drawing board. Cars become design disasters for many different reasons. Some are just fundamentally terrible designs, flawed in a number of ways and often lacking an element that would seem far too obvious for most people to omit. Why didn't the Austin Princess have a hatchback, for example? And why did the FSO Polonez come with a hatch, but no fold-down rear seat? These are questions that have never been answered.

Others are disastrous because they lacked mechanical detail. They were fairly adventurous, but failed because they hadn't been properly thought out. Then there are those whose design faults are instantly evident—if it's true that a car's design appeal starts with its styling, travesties such as the AMC Gremlin, Pontiac Aztek and Subaru XT Coupé should never have come into being . . .

Left: *The Mercedes Vaneo—proof that even today, car makers can get it horribly wrong sometimes.*

AUSTIN AMBASSADOR *(1982–84)*

It didn't take long for British Leyland to realize that the original Princess should have been given a hatchback rather than a conventional trunk, and a redesign started within months of the car going into production. It finally arrived in showrooms in 1982 as the Austin Ambassador, complete with an aerodynamic front end and folding rear seats to accommodate long loads. To cut costs, it used the same platform, doors and suspension system as the Princess, and shared its distinctive wedge-shaped profile.

But this was too little too late. By the time it arrived, the Ambassador was a dead duck. It was outdated compared to most modern rivals, and the atrocious 1.7-liter and 2.0-liter O-Series engines were notoriously fragile and started burning oil at less than 20,000 miles (32,200km). Top of the range was a Vanden Plas model, with a sumptuous interior and a unique radiator grille—a cynical attempt to sell it as an executive car.

 AUSTIN AMBASSADOR
Expensive motor cars-in all but price.

AUSTIN

Left: "Expensive motor cars in all but price." And build quality. And style. And performance. And reliability. And image. Need we go on?

Two power units were offered in the Ambassador, either a 104ci (1.7-liter) or 122ci (2.0-liter) O-Series overhead cam engine. Both were unrefined and dreadfully unreliable.

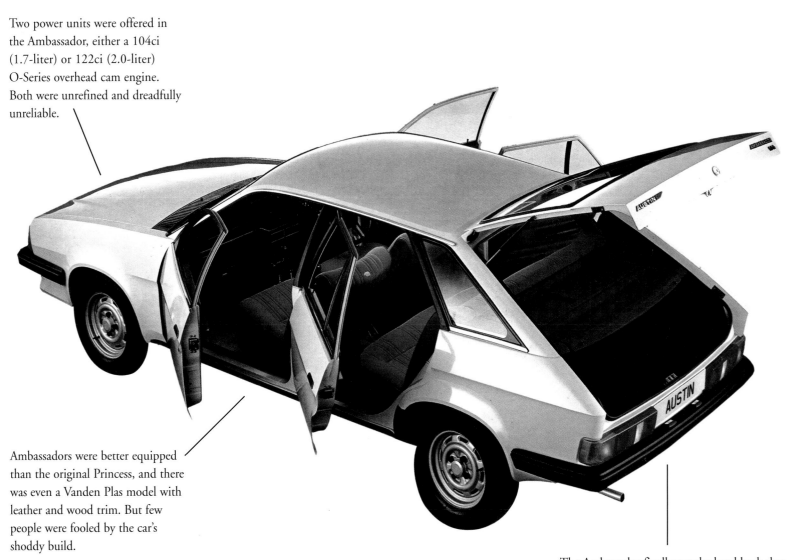

Ambassadors were better equipped than the original Princess, and there was even a Vanden Plas model with leather and wood trim. But few people were fooled by the car's shoddy build.

The Ambassador finally got the hatchback that was missing from the Princess, but this was barely compensated, as the original wedge's lines were ruined by the new look.

CITROËN GS BIROTOR (1974–75)

Given its reputation for unusual and creative design, it's hardly surprising that Citroën was one of the first manufacturers to jump on the rotary engine bandwagon. It joined forces with German firm NSU to develop a range of twin rotary "Wankel" engines in 1967, but the relationship didn't last long and the company—Comotor—was disbanded soon afterward. Citroën persisted, though, and the GS Birotor finally arrived in 1974. It was an enterprising idea—but ultimately a disaster. The GS Birotor was fast and stylish, but it was considerably more expensive than a four-cylinder variant and suffered from wear to the rotor seal tips, causing premature engine failure.

In the end, Citroën gave up on the project after selling just 847 examples. Most of them were bought back by Citroën and destroyed, as the French firm didn't want to deal with the issue of having to maintain a parts network.

SPECIFICATIONS

TOP SPEED:	109mph (175km/h)
0–60MPH (0–96KM/H):	14.0secs
ENGINE TYPE:	twin rotary Wankel
DISPLACEMENT:	2 x 30ci (2 x 497.5cc)
WEIGHT:	2600lb (1170kg)
MILEAGE:	22mpg (12.8l/100km)

Left: *This diagram shows how the rotary engine worked—but wear to the rotor tips caused it to lose all compression.*

The Birotor was identical to the standard GS in terms of its styling—the only differences were a couple of extra cooling ducts in the front and discreet "Birotor" badges.

Handling and performance were excellent thanks to the GS's light weight, but the rotary engine was inefficient and thirsty.

Citroën's tie-in with Comotor resulted in the GS being offered with rotary power, but as with all early rotary engines the unit was fragile and prone to premature failure.

FIAT MULTIPLA *(1998–2004)*

When it appeared in 1998, the Fiat Multipla caused quite a stir. Its styling challenged convention, and, although it was actually a decent people-carrier in most respects, its bizarre looks were enough to scare off the majority of buyers. Even Fiat was prepared to confess that the Multipla wasn't exactly beautiful—press demonstration cars in the UK came with a sticker in the rear window that read: "Wait until you see the front!"

Car journalists raved about the Multipla's clever three-abreast seating arrangement, immense practicality and excellent driving position, but ultimately it was doomed to failure because buyers weren't brave enough to part with their cash. The Italian firm finally gave up with the Multipla's quirkiness in 2004, and restyled the nose and tail to give it a far more conventional, if less intriguing, appearance.

SPECIFICATIONS

TOP SPEED:	107mph (173km/h)
0–60MPH (0–96KM/H):	12.6secs
ENGINE TYPE:	in-line four
DISPLACEMENT:	96ci (1581cc)
WEIGHT:	3266lb (1470kg)
MILEAGE:	34mpg (8.3l/100km)

Left: Although it appeared much larger, the Multipla was based on the platform of the Bravo/Brava range of family hatchbacks, with the track increased to give greater width.

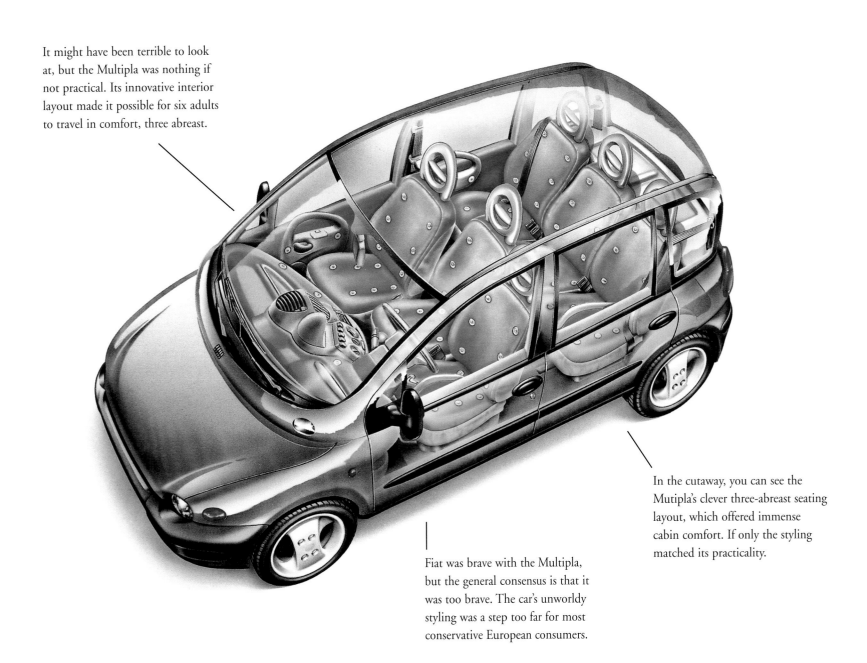

It might have been terrible to look at, but the Multipla was nothing if not practical. Its innovative interior layout made it possible for six adults to travel in comfort, three abreast.

In the cutaway, you can see the Mutipla's clever three-abreast seating layout, which offered immense cabin comfort. If only the styling matched its practicality.

Fiat was brave with the Multipla, but the general consensus is that it was too brave. The car's unworldy styling was a step too far for most conservative European consumers.

FORD CLASSIC/CAPRI 109E (1961–64)

There was certainly nothing wrong with the styling of Ford's new family contender for 1961. The Classic bore several U.S. design influences and looked fantastic, with its distinctive grille, quad headlights and reverse-raked rear window. The two-door Capri coupé looked even prettier, but the 109E series was a definite case of beauty being only skin deep. In Ford terms, the Classic and Capri were disasters—expensive to develop, difficult to build and slow sellers in a marketplace where buyers favored more traditional designs. There were also problems with the original three-bearing engine, which was prone to premature big-end failure. And despite those alluring looks, neither was great to drive, with sluggish acceleration and heavy bodywork that caused the skinny tires to lose grip prematurely. Production lasted just three years before the Cortina appeared, with far more success.

SPECIFICATIONS

TOP SPEED:	95mph (153km/h)
0–60MPH (0–96KM/H):	13.7secs
ENGINE TYPE:	in-line four
DISPLACEMENT:	82ci (1340cc)
WEIGHT:	1995lb (898kg)
MILEAGE:	28mpg (10.0l/100km)

Left: We haven't got a clue why there's a woman sitting on a deckchair in the trunk of this Capri 109E. Perhaps the driver ran out of seats inside?

The first 109Es had an engine with just three main bearings. As the cars were heavy, the engines had to be worked hard, and premature wear to the front end was common.

The fluted wings, incorporating the indicator lights, were touted as a styling feature of the 109E. But while they looked good, they provided a convenient rust trap, from which the rest of the front structure would rot out.

It might have looked sporty, but the 109E wasn't a particularly dynamic car to drive. The weight made the handling difficult, and performance was never great.

FSO POLONEZ/CARO *(1985–98)*

After Fiat withdrew from FSO on the grounds that its association with the Polish brand did its reputation few favors, the company was left to develop a new car—the Polonez. Despite entirely new bodywork, it still used an archaic suspension setup and a 1500cc Fiat engine, built under license from the Italian maker. In styling terms, it wasn't pretty, even if its trapezoid profile and twin-headlight grille were in keeping with contemporary styling from other European makers. But it had precious little to recommend it. The handling was terrifying, the quality was atrocious and the use of ultra-cheap paint meant that most Polonezes rotted away early on. Then there was that fundamental design flaw in a hatchback—the rear seat didn't drop. The car was briefly revived as the Caro in the early 1990s, this time using Peugeot engines, but it was hardly any better.

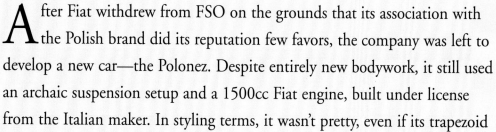

SPECIFICATIONS

TOP SPEED:	93mph (150km/h)
0–60MPH (0–96KM/H):	18.8secs
ENGINE TYPE:	in-line four
DISPLACEMENT:	90ci (1481cc)
WEIGHT:	2459lb (1106kg)
MILEAGE:	28mpg
	(10.0l/100km)

Left: It's sunset, and the owner of this Polonez still hasn't managed to get the thing started. Looks like he's here for the evening . . .

Cabins were awful—the design lacked any kind of logic, plastics were cheap, and although the Polonez had a hatchback, the rear seat couldn't be folded, leaving it with a tiny trunk.

FSO couldn't afford to develop its own engine, so the Polonez had an engine carried over from the Fiat 125 and dating back to the 1950s.

It was designed for rough Eastern European roads, so the Polonez sat high off the ground. That gave it dreadful balance problems on smoother Western European roads.

HILLMAN IMP *(1963–76)*

Had Hillman not left its customers to do the development work after the car went on sale, the Imp could have been one of the great success stories of the British motor industry. Sadly it wasn't, and the blame could be apportioned equally between the manufacturer and the British government. Rootes Group was given a substantial sum to invest in a new factory in Linwood, Scotland, where unemployment was rife, and a staff of ex-shipbuilders was brought in to assemble the Imp. Then workers got wind that their colleagues in Coventry earned more, and militant unionism meant that both build quality and development suffered. But Rootes had arranged a date for the first car to come off the line, with the Duke of Edinburgh booked to drive it, so the car was hurried into production unfinished and the earliest examples were shockingly unreliable.

SPECIFICATIONS

TOP SPEED:	80mph (130km/h)
0–60MPH (0–96KM/H):	25.4secs
ENGINE TYPE:	in-line four
DISPLACEMENT:	53ci (875cc)
WEIGHT:	1530lb (688kg)
MILEAGE:	37mpg (7.6l/100km)

Left: If test-driving an Imp was "an amazing experience that you owe yourself," then what must it have been like to drive an infinitely better car?

Test-drive an IMP – it's an amazing experience you owe yourself

HERE'S FULL-SIZE FAMILY MOTORING WITH REAL PERFORMANCE, RELIABILITY AND SUPERB ECONOMY

★ TAKES FOUR WITHOUT SQUASH, FUSS OR EFFORT
Easily takes four adults—with luggage—in extreme comfort. Back window lifts up, rear seat folds down to give estate car convenience.

★ OUTSTANDING FUEL ECONOMY OF 40 SERVICE COSTS
Touring consumption of 40-45 m.p.g. (higher still with careful driving). No greasing; routine service once every 5000 miles.

★ SUPERB TRACTION UNDER ALL ROAD CONDITIONS
Balanced weight distribution over all four 12" wheels. First-class road-holding.

★ ACCELERATION THAT PUTS OTHERS IN THE REAR-VIEW MIRROR
875 c.c. 0-50 m.p.h. in 15 seconds. Up to 80 m.p.h.

★ SAFETY IN SUSPENSION—SAFETY IN BRAKING
Independent suspension. Big brakes take the strain of hard braking without any sign of fade.

★ ALUMINIUM OVERHEAD CAM ENGINE, ALL-SYNCHROMESH GEARS
Lightweight rear engine gives a high performance economically and effortlessly. 4-speed synchromesh gear box.

IMP Saloon £420 plus p.t. IMP de Luxe £440 plus p.t. IMP de Luxe has heater and unique 'thru-flow' ventilation, screen-washers, opening quarter lights, four stowage pockets, fully-carpeted floor, twin sun-visors, safety belt anchor points all included. Whitewall tyres and overriders available as extras.

AN IMP FOR £3. 3. 10. A WEEK

Through the hire purchase terms offered by ROOTES ACCEPTANCES LIMITED:—
Cash price (Ex Works) £506 1 3
Initial payment £101 18 3
36 monthly payments, each of £13 16 7

Modern design and styling will maintain Imp's high resale value for years to come

HILLMAN IMP
MAKE A DATE WITH AN IMP TODAY!

Made in Scotland by ROOTES MOTORS LIMITED

HILLMAN MOTOR CAR CO LTD · DIVISION OF ROOTES MOTORS LIMITED · LONDON COACHWORKS AND EXPORT DIVISION: ROOTES LIMITED · DEVONSHIRE HOUSE · PICCADILLY · LONDON W.I

Among its many clever features, the Imp had a hinged rear window that provided extra storage space behind the rear seat. If only it had been better built, it could have been a success.

The spare wheel lived under the hood. With the engine at the rear, it gave weight to the front of the car and helped balance the handling.

It was the shoddy build quality that killed the Imp. As well as leaking water, the car rusted drastically, especially around the front firewall and door bottoms.

PUY 249L

MERCEDES VANEO *(2001–present)*

In recent years, Mercedes has gone to great lengths to ensure that it has a car available in every imaginable market sector. And while some of these niches have been a remarkable success for the company—notably the supermini-sized A-Class and SLK Roadster—it has always taken shortcuts with its MPVs. The enormous van-based V-Class was bad enough, but the smaller Vaneo was a particularly poor attempt by Mercedes at cashing in on a lucrative market sector.

Even though it isn't a van, it looks like one, while the name does it no favors, implying that it is a commercial vehicle pretending to be a family car. The engines are underpowered and handling abilities are distinctively average, while inside the Vaneo seems to lack both the quality and integrity that have long been Mercedes hallmarks. It's not surprising, then, that the Vaneo's sales success proved somewhat limited.

Left: The Vaneo may look like a van from the outside, but the interior is as luxurious as any Mercedes-Benz. That's certainly no reason for buying one, though.

Engines come from the Mercedes A-Class, and, while these are fine in a small car, they lack performance in the Vaneo and aren't especially efficient.

Despite its name, the Mercedes Vaneo isn't actually based on a van. So why did the stylists make it look like one?

The Vaneo offers plenty of space, and there's even a seven-seater version. But it's far too expensive, and rivals from Citroën, Peugeot, and Fiat do the job so much better.

MINI CLUBMAN *(1969–81)*

You can't improve on perfection, and the Mini Clubman is all the evidence you'll ever need. It was launched in 1969 as a supposed update to the then 10-year-old Mini, and, in creating the Clubman, British Leyland's designers took the original Alec Issigonis shape and modified it to wear the company's new corporate nose, shared with the unspectacular Maxi. In essence, it wasn't such a bad idea—after all, the original Mini's engine bay was cramped, which made it difficult to work on. But whoever was responsible for the redesign was unsympathetic toward the original Mini's gorgeous looks, and the Clubman appeared too long, while the squared-off nose sat awkwardly with the curvaceous tail inherited from the standard Mini. After twelve years of production, where it sold alongside the original car, the Clubman was shelved and the original continued.

SPECIFICATIONS

TOP SPEED:	90mph (145km/h)
0–60MPH (0–96KM/H):	13.3secs
ENGINE TYPE:	in-line four
DISPLACEMENT:	78ci (1275cc)
WEIGHT:	1555lb (699kg)
MILEAGE:	40mpg (7.0l/100km)

Left: *While Britain may indeed be small, driving from one end to the other in a Mini Clubman remains a deeply uncomfortable experience.*

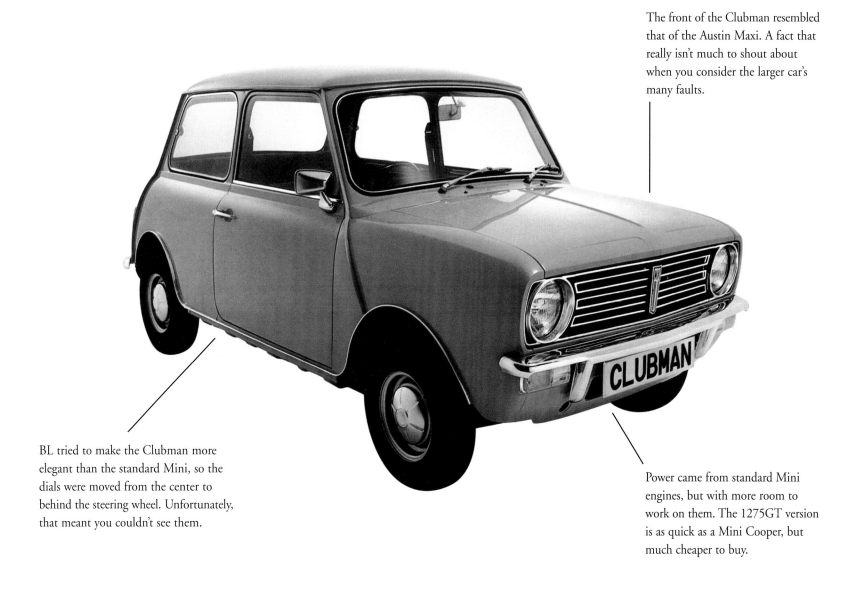

The front of the Clubman resembled that of the Austin Maxi. A fact that really isn't much to shout about when you consider the larger car's many faults.

BL tried to make the Clubman more elegant than the standard Mini, so the dials were moved from the center to behind the steering wheel. Unfortunately, that meant you couldn't see them.

Power came from standard Mini engines, but with more room to work on them. The 1275GT version is as quick as a Mini Cooper, but much cheaper to buy.

RENAULT AVANTIME *(2002–2003)*

There's something quite alluring about the Renault Avantime, despite it being remembered as one of the biggest flops of recent car history. The car was doomed to failure by its very concept. Using the platform of the Renault Espace people-carrier, the French manufacturer decided to build a coupé with a hint of the Espace in its styling. What finally arrived after four years of planning was utterly pointless.

It was huge on the outside, yet barely big enough inside to seat four people. The two-door bodyshell used enormous doors, which were too big to open in a tight parking space, and the out-of-this-world styling turned many a head, but not necessarily for the right reasons. When coachbuilder Matra, which built the Avantime for Renault, went bust in 2003, the model was canned for good—after less than a year in production. A disaster, though in design terms, a very brave effort.

SPECIFICATIONS

TOP SPEED:	138mph (222km/h)
0–60MPH (0–96KM/H):	8.6secs
ENGINE TYPE:	V6
DISPLACEMENT:	180ci (2946cc)
WEIGHT:	3868lb (1741kg)
MILEAGE:	25mpg (11.3l/100km)

Left: The Avantime certainly isn't large once you climb inside, even if it does look large. There's only room for four, and those in the back need short legs.

38

Despite its huge dimensions, rear legroom was cramped in the back of the Renault Avantime, as the cutaway drawing at right clearly shows.

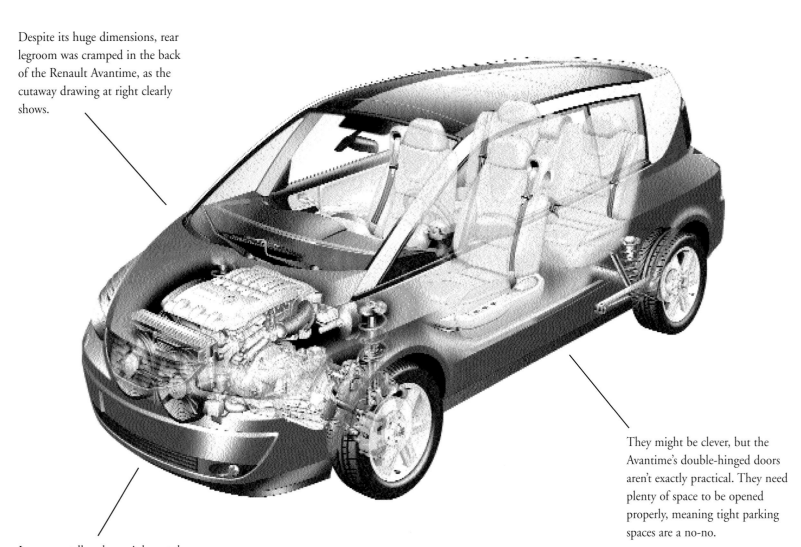

They might be clever, but the Avantime's double-hinged doors aren't exactly practical. They need plenty of space to be opened properly, meaning tight parking spaces are a no-no.

It appears tall and ungainly, yet the Avantime's lightweight fiberglass bodywork makes for surprisingly agile handling and a low center of gravity.

VOLVO 340 *(1975–92)*

When is a Volvo not a Volvo? Answer: When it's built in Holland by a truck manufacturer. The ugly 340 series was originally planned to replace the DAF 66, but, when Volvo took over the Dutch firm in 1975, it launched it as its own. Engines were bought under license from Renault and were the same units that powered the Renault 5, 9 and 11, meaning they were reliable but unrefined.

The gearbox was mounted above the rear axle, necessitating the use of an extraordinarily long linkage and ruining the gear shift. Handling was stodgy, and rear shocks were years behind most independently sprung rivals. And yet, awful as it was, the 340 was a tremendous sales success. Especially in the UK market, where it remained in the top 10 bestseller lists right up to its death in 1992, by which time it had become a million-seller.

SPECIFICATIONS

TOP SPEED:	94mph (152km/h)
0–60MPH (0–96KM/H):	15.0secs
ENGINE TYPE:	in-line four
DISPLACEMENT:	85ci (1397cc)
WEIGHT:	2184lb (983kg)
MILEAGE:	35mpg (7.8l/100km)

Left: *Volvo's reputation for safety was carried over into the 340, and this illustration shows what the crumple zones did in an accident.*

It was launched at a similar time to classics such as the VW Golf, but the 340 didn't follow traditional hatchback styling cues. In fact, it was a very odd shape.

Power came from a range of outdated overhead valve Renault engines, so performance and refinement weren't great. That said, they're impossible to kill.

There was nothing modern about the 340's suspension. Shocks at the rear and struts at the front made it tail-happy, especially given the rear-drive layout.

FINANCIAL FAILURES

When it comes to a car being a flop, it's fair to say that a car that bankrupts its manufacturer is a pretty spectacular dud. And many of the vehicles in this section did just that—huge development costs, appalling sales records and a complete lack of showroom appeal meant their makers could never recoup the enormous investment required to bring a car to market. The likes of Bricklin, De Lorean, Edsel and Tucker may never see the light of day again, but there will be other ambitious car builders who grind to a halt, stalled by their own attempts to succeed in one of the most cut-throat industries in the world.

Some cars were reasonably good sellers—the Austin 1100, for example, sold over a million in its 11-year life. But British Leyland lost money on every single car it built. In mass production terms, that's a huge loss. And BL was not alone, as Lancia and Chrysler will testify.

Some entries here did not lose money themselves, but acquired such an appalling reputation that the damage they did to their makers' reputations meant the losses suffered later on were immense.

Left: *The AC 3000 ME was out of date by the time it reached production, and nearly crippled the company that built it.*

AC 3000 ME (1979–84)

With the legendary Cobra in its bloodline, the AC 3000 ME should have been a success story. Here, promised the company, was the Cobra's spiritual successor: an affordable two-seater sports car with a lively rear-drive chassis and a powerful Ford engine. The car was first shown at the 1973 London Motor Show as the Diablo, and received rave reviews—it was cited as Britain's first affordable supercar. But things quickly went downhill. It took another six years for the 3000 ME to reach production, by which time the price had leapt to more than three times the proposed price. It was horrifically expensive and complicated to build, the handling was terrible and the performance wasn't even all that good. Oh, and it also suffered gearbox problems. It cost millions to develop and practically crippled the company, and only 82 cars were ever built before AC was forced into receivership.

SPECIFICATIONS

TOP SPEED:	120mph (193km/h)
0–60MPH (0–96KM/H):	8.5secs
ENGINE TYPE:	V6
DISPLACEMENT:	182ci (2994cc)
WEIGHT:	2483lb (1117kg)
MILEAGE:	18mpg (16.6l/100km)

Left: The marketing campaigns were boastful, but not impressive enough to secure sufficient sales to keep the AC 3000 ME in production.

AC made its own gear linkages to mate to the Ford engine, and this became the model's biggest downfall, with frequent gearbox failure.

Power came from a Ford V6 engine mounted in the middle of the chassis, but, despite this layout, weight distribution was poor and the handling was never great.

The 3000 ME used a fiberglass body mounted on a complex sheet steel chassis, the two combining to make it difficult—and expensive—to build.

AUSTIN GIPSY (1958–68)

With the immeasurable success of the Land Rover, the Austin Gipsy was hastily rushed into production so that BMC could earn itself part of the large crust that came out of mobilizing Britain's military troops. The Gipsy looked almost identical to a Land Rover, but came with a complex—and expensive—rubber based suspension system. It was effective at first, but reliability and rust problems came to light, and it simply wasn't tough enough to satisfy the demands of armed forces, meaning it failed to recoup its development costs. When Rover (and consequently Land Rover) joined the British Leyland Motor Corporation in 1968, it became surplus to requirements, and was swept under the carpet as an expensive mistake, best forgotten.

SPECIFICATIONS

TOP SPEED:	68mph (110km/h)
0–60MPH (0–96KM/H):	no figures available
ENGINE TYPE:	in-line four
DISPLACEMENT:	133ci (2188cc)
WEIGHT:	3360lb (1512kg)
MILEAGE:	20mpg (14.1l/100km)

Left: *The Gipsy was intended as a rugged, easy-to-fix military vehicle, so what did BMC use in its publicity photographs? Why, an elegant woman, of course.*

The suspension was made out of rubber, which gave it flexibility and a good ride when new, but, as the rubber aged and perished, the ride and handling became terrible.

Unlike its arch rival, the Land Rover, the Gipsy used steel panels instead of aluminum. That made it prone to rot, especially if used in damp conditions.

The 134ci (2.2-liter) engine was fairly powerful, but was geared for torque rather than performance. That gave the Gipsy immense pulling power, but a low top speed.

BOND BUG (1970–74)

B ritain's two biggest manufacturers of fiberglass cars merged in the late 1960s, with Reliant taking over struggling Bond. It saw the move as a way of experimenting with some fairly adventurous designs without putting Reliant's reputation at risk, and the first and only fruit was this—the completely bonkers Bug. Available only in dayglow orange, the Bug looked like a garishly colored doorstop on three wheels.

It enjoyed limited success, but most buyers found it far too ludicrous for their tastes and it was dropped after four years and a build run of just over 2,000 cars. The Bond name had become a joke associated with the mad Bug, and it was never reintroduced, its reputa-

tion irrevocably tarnished. Yet despite killing its maker, the Bug enjoys a remarkable survival rate, with almost half of those built still on the road!

Left: *You can have any color as long as it's orange! Henry Ford would have been turning in his grave at the prospect of Bond's unique paint scheme. Plenty of space for those important documents, though.*

To climb inside the Bug, you pulled a latch at the front, whereupon the roof and windshield lifted away, providing access to the driver's seat.

The rear-mounted alloy engine was taken from Reliant, and gave the Bug what was a surprisingly peppy performance.

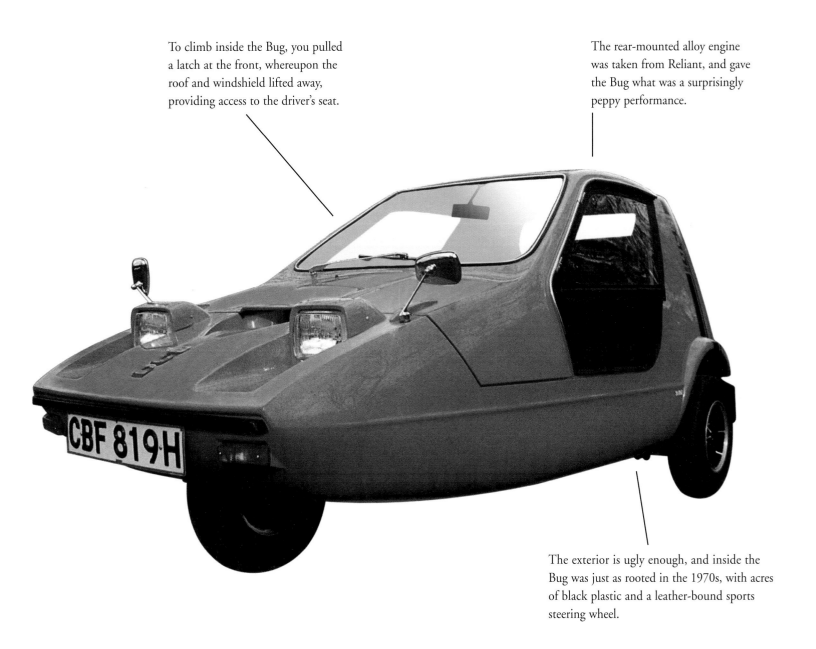

CBF 819 H

The exterior is ugly enough, and inside the Bug was just as rooted in the 1970s, with acres of black plastic and a leather-bound sports steering wheel.

BRICKLIN SV-1 (1974–75)

Canadian entrepreneur Malcolm Bricklin was so confident that his proposed "Safety Sports Car" would be a huge success that he provided $23 million to build the factory for it, securing the backing of the country's government along the way. The fiberglass-bodied car debuted in 1974 and looked quite stylish, with wedge-shaped lines and gullwing doors—but it was ultimately doomed to failure. Reliability was poor, the AMC-sourced engines were appalling and build quality was dreadful: several owners were trapped inside when the doors locked up. Fewer than 3,000 (or a tenth of Malcolm Bricklin's prediction) were built in the first year, and the project collapsed, swallowing all of Bricklin's money and resulting in severe recriminations at government level. One of the auto industry's biggest failures.

SPECIFICATIONS

TOP SPEED:	122mph (196km/h)
0–60MPH (0–96KM/H):	8.5secs
ENGINE TYPE:	V8
DISPLACEMENT:	360ci (5899cc)
WEIGHT:	3530lb (1600kg)
MILEAGE:	19mpg
	(14.9l/100km)

Left: *The creator of the SV-1—the Canadian inventor and businessman, Malcolm Bricklin—whose dream never became a success.*

If the battery died, the gullwing doors wouldn't open, meaning the only way to escape was to clamber out of the rear hatch.

The Bricklin was made out of fiberglass, but this wasn't bonded properly, which meant it cracked and warped during climate extremes.

SV stood for "Safety Vehicle," and that meant it got a distinctly unpleasant lip on the front of the wedge-shaped nose, making it look like it had suffered an accident.

DAF 33/DAFFODIL *(1967–75)*

The Netherlands has never had much of a car industry, but it did have one sales success. That car was the Daffodil, or 33, and more than 300,000 were sold in an eight-year production run. It was a fascinating piece of automotive engineering, offering compact but spacious transport at a sensible price. However, it also had an interesting transmission, made of a series of belt-driven cones attached to the axles and split by a centrifugal clutch. As a result, it was unnecessarily expensive to build, leading to several financial problems for the company that wouldn't be overcome until Swedish maker Volvo took over the helm in 1975, writing off Daf's massive debts.

Perhaps the Daffodil's most intriguing aspect was that, thanks to the transmission, it could go just as quickly in reverse as it could when driven forward! In truth, though, it was a terrible car that wrecked the company that built it.

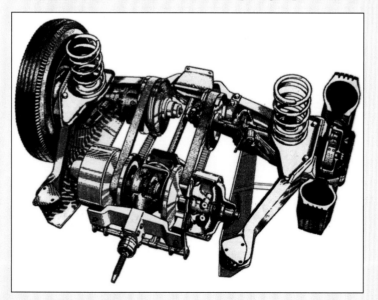

SPECIFICATIONS

TOP SPEED:	50mph (80km/h)
0–60MPH (0–96KM/H):	not possible
ENGINE TYPE:	flat-twin
DISPLACEMENT:	36ci (590cc)
WEIGHT:	1268lb (571kg)
MILEAGE:	40mpg (7.0l/100km)

Left: *This blow-up diagram of the rear transaxle shows how the Daf 33 used a centrifugal clutch and unusual belt-driven transmission.*

Amazingly, the 33's handling was really quite good. It was no larger than a BMC Mini and used the same wheel-at-each-corner philosophy.

This was no performance car. It used a 36ci (590cc) flat-twin engine, and struggled to top 50mph (80km/h) at full speed.

The Daf 33 didn't so much have a gearbox as a direct linkage from the engine to the wheels via a series of rubber belts. It was as fast going backward as it was going forward.

DE LOREAN DMC 12 *(1981–82)*

One of the most documented failures in motoring, the De Lorean found fame as the car-based time machine in the *Back to the Future* films. But its screen success wasn't matched in the showrooms, and the car was a total flop. The brainchild of ex-Pontiac man John Z. De Lorean, it was built in Northern Ireland, where many hopes were pinned on its success. It was funded by government money, with a chassis by Lotus and styling by Giugiaro. But it was awful. Quality was dire, the stainless-steel body panels were easily marked, and the performance and handling were poor. It bombed, foundering in a trail of debt, corruption, and job losses, with accusations of embezzlement, backhanders, and bribery among the project's management. And millions of pounds of British taxpayers' money went down the drain with it.

SPECIFICATIONS

TOP SPEED:	121mph (194km/h)
0–60MPH (0–96KM/H):	10.2secs
ENGINE TYPE:	V6
DISPLACEMENT:	174ci (2849cc)
WEIGHT:	3093lb (1392kg)
MILEAGE:	24mpg
	(11.8l/100km)

Left: The DMC 12 might have been the subject of various untruths and cover-ups, but De Lorean certainly wasn't lying when it claimed the car had "distinctive looks from any direction!"

For some reason, De Lorean chose a
Renault V6 engine for the DMC-12.
It was heavy and made handling
tricky, without offering any major
performance benefits.

The car's brushed stainless-steel
panels had no structural purpose—
purely for effect, they covered
fiberglass items.

The gullwing doors were a design
feature purely for show, and they
weren't properly engineered, often
trapping passengers inside the car.

MISPLACED MARQUES

The concept of "badge engineering," or branding one car as another, has been around since the late 1950s, when the British Motor Corporation took six versions of the same car and put different names on each one, in a bid to cash in on buyers' brand loyalty. It became a global trend, with several other manufacturers following suit. There was a point when buying a Chrysler, Dodge or Plymouth, or a Chevrolet, Pontiac or Buick, got you essentially the same car with a different name on the front. Some of the cars in the following pages show badge engineering taken to shameful extremes.

There have been such cynical naming exercises as a Nissan Cherry with an Alfa Romeo shield on its grille, a downmarket Kia with Ford's blue oval on its nose, and possibly the worst ever misinterpretation of MG's revered octagon, when Austin-Rover saw fit to glue it onto an especially nasty Maestro. Other entries are simply old, outdated models, given new names and marketed in different countries to try to eke out the last ounces of profitability from aging tooling.

Left: *Many marques live on long after they've been forgotten in their domestic markets.*
The Paykan is Iran's take on the Hillman Hunter.

PORSCHE CAYENNE *(2003–present)*

From a driver's perspective, it's true, there's nothing wrong with the Porsche Cayenne. It's powerful, has remarkable handling for an SUV and is well built. But there's so much wrong with the ideology behind it that Porsche purists despise the model—and not without good reason. The most obvious flaw is the styling. It's far from elegant, with an awkward mix of traditional Porsche styling cues and the slab-sided profile that's endemic of any off-road machine.

Then there's the cynicism—the Cayenne was built so that people could have lots of kids and still own a Porsche, which is hardly the reason so many owners scrimp and save to get their hands on one. Finally, it was developed alongside the VW Touareg and even shares its entry-level six-cylinder engine. Unless you have to have the Porsche badge, the VW is a far better buy all round.

SPECIFICATIONS

TOP SPEED:	155mph (266k/mh)
0–60MPH (0–96KM/H):	5.6secs
ENGINE TYPE:	V8 turbo
DISPLACEMENT:	275ci (4511cc)
WEIGHT:	3650lb (2355kg)
MILEAGE:	21mpg
	(13.4l/100km)

Left: *The cutaway drawing clearly shows the Cayenne's springing system and transmission layout, both of which are identical to those offered on the VW Touareg.*

The Cayenne claims to be a Porsche—but the vehicle has the same doors as the VW Touareg, and under the skin is essentially the same architecture.

Cayennes have a V8 engine that's purely Porsche designed—and it's a cracker. But entry-level cars come with a 195ci (3.2-liter) Volkswagen V6 and, despite the Porsche branding, they're not even that fast.

Whatever angle you look at it from, the Cayenne's styling is challenging. The lines aren't harmonious, and some writers have compared the car's bulbous nose and huge air intake to the face of a wide-mouthed toad.

For a car so large and tall, the Cayenne has good levels of grip and assured handling. But the downside is an incredibly harsh ride, which transmits every jolt from the suspension upward into the cabin.

59

TRIUMPH ACCLAIM *(1981–84)*

The Acclaim was a critical car for the British motor industry, as it marked the first tie-in between what was then British Leyland (later Rover) and Japanese maker Honda—an alliance that would go on to save the company in the following decade. But the Acclaim certainly wasn't the car to stop the rot that was the result of years of pandering to trade unions. It was based on the Honda Ballade, a four-door sedan popular in Japan and America. If BL had badged the car as an Austin or Morris, it would probably have been a success, but instead they chose to put the mark of upmarket brand Triumph on the nose and tail.

Most Triumph buyers were used to luxurious small cars, and the Acclaim's plastic cabin and bland Japanese styling just weren't their cup of tea. The model was scrapped after two years.

SPECIFICATIONS

TOP SPEED:	92mph (148km/h)
0–60MPH (0–96KM/H):	12.9secs
ENGINE TYPE:	in-line four
DISPLACEMENT:	81ci (1335cc)
MILEAGE:	8.3l/100km (34mpg)

Left: *"The Acclaim beats all comers," says Triumph, referring to such mighty adversaries as the Renault 9 and Ford Escort Mk 3, but conveniently forgetting good cars such as the VW Golf and anything Japanese.*

Triumph purists liked rear wheel drive and firm suspension, neither of which the Acclaim could offer. It had soft springs, front-wheel drive and little in the way of handling prowess, with a chassis prone to understeer and sloppy steering response.

Triumphs were always upmarket and well appointed, so the Acclaim was a disappointment to the brand's traditional buyers. Gone were the upmarket wood and leather, to be replaced by velour upholstery and a plastic dashboard.

Although it had Japanese reliability engineered in, the Acclaim could still rust in the same way that British cars always had done. So the rear wheel arches rotted out, the doors went crusty and the sills gave way.

Power was provided by tough and reliable Honda engines, so the news wasn't all bad. But Triumph offered its own Trio-Matic three-speed auto transmission, which was especially slow to respond and delivered dire performance.

ASIA ROCSTA (1993–95)

There have been several Jeep clones over the years, but one of the least subtle copies was the Asia Rocsta, introduced by Korean company Kia in 1986. The Rocsta was originally built for South Korea's military forces, and by the early 1990s was introduced into certain markets as a leisure vehicle, capitalizing on the growth of the potent SUV market in Europe. But while it looked fairly cool, the Rocsta was truly awful. It came with a choice of either a 1.8-liter pushrod gasoline engine or a smoky old Peugeot-sourced diesel, neither of which offered any performance.

The ride was harsh, the steering was bad and quality was terrible. Buyers might have overlooked this if the car had been an established brand, but the Asia Motors name was new to European markets and meant nothing to potential customers.

SPECIFICATIONS	
TOP SPEED:	70mph (113km/h)
0–60MPH (0–96KM/H):	36.5secs
ENGINE TYPE:	in-line four
DISPLACEMENT:	105ci (1789cc)
WEIGHT:	3748lb (1700kg)
MILEAGE:	25mpg
	(11.3l/100km)

Left: *Considering the car's poor handling and bumpy ride, Asia Motors was correct to claim the Rocsta was not for the faint of heart!*

Handling was terrible: the live rear axle and leaf spring combination meant the Rocsta was prone to rolling over, while the vehicle's uncompromising ride jarred occupants' spines.

The interior quality was perhaps the Rocsta's biggest fault. The plastics were awful, the driving position uncomfortable, and the column stalks used to snap off.

Power—if you could call it that—came from a choice of outdated Mitsubishi gasoline or Peugeot diesel engines.

N444 RCS

LIGIER AMBRA *(1998–present)*

There's a strong market in France for small four-wheeled vehicles with an engine capacity of less than 500cc. The Ambra is one such car, as a dispensation in the law allows them to be driven by people who don't have driver's licenses, often from as young as 14 years of age. That's a terrifying prospect when you consider just how difficult the Ambra is to drive.

The cabin is impossible to sit comfortably in, the brakes do a very poor impression of actually working, and the handling is terrifying. Approach the same corner several times at the same speed, and each time the Ambra will handle differently. This is a truly, truly awful motor car that is deeply unpleasant in almost every respect.

Country and GLX version

SPECIFICATIONS

TOP SPEED:	62mph (100km/h)
0–60MPH (0–96KM/H):	no figures available
ENGINE TYPE:	flat-twin
DISPLACEMENT:	31ci (505cc)
WEIGHT:	no figure available
MILEAGE:	60mpg (4.7l/100km)

Left: *According to the advertisement, the Ambra came in both "Country" and luxury versions, both of them horrible to drive.*

You need to be fairly athletic to get comfortable in the Ambra. The driving position is terrible, with the pedals offset to the right, and a lack of seat adjustment makes it impossible for tall people to get comfortable inside.

You know the Ambra is a bad car as soon as you turn it on. The engine is crude and noisy, and there's hardly any soundproofing. Acceleration is also dreadfully slow.

It's just as well that the Ambra can't go very quickly because the handling is appalling. It has no front-end grip, the steering lacks any kind of feel and the basic suspension setup causes it to lurch and wallow around bends.

MASERATI BITURBO *(1981–91)*

Maserati tried to go more conventional than usual with the Biturbo, and introduced a car that was cheaper and more ordinary-looking than previous offerings. It was supposed to take on the likes of the BMW 635 and Jaguar XJS, but actually it looked stupid. For starters, there was the styling: boring, like an early 1980s American sedan rather than a sports coupé. The only saving grace was a beautifully ornate interior. That wasn't enough, though, as the Biturbo suffered from horrendous turbo lag.

It was slow off the mark, then the V6 engine's twin turbos could kick in with dramatic effect. Coupled to the rather crude chassis, this made it prone to oversteering, especially if the turbos came in mid-turn.

SPECIFICATIONS

TOP SPEED:	126mph (203km/h)
0–60MPH (0–96KM/H):	7.3secs
ENGINE TYPE:	V6
DISPLACEMENT:	152ci (2491cc)
WEIGHT:	2739lb (1233kg)
MILEAGE:	25mpg (11.3l/100km)

Left: A self-proclaimed "modern day classic" according to Maserati, but someone obviously forgot to tell the styling department.

Maserati tried a less dramatic approach when styling the Biturbo, but instead of creating a car that was elegant in its simplicity the designers came up with a generic design that looked far too much like a Chrylser Le Baron.

Italian luxury opulence was very much in evidence, with beautiful hand-stitched leather seat facings, suede detailing, and gold-edge dashboard dials.

Handling was terrible: with appalling turbo lag and a crude suspension setup, the Biturbo couldn't cope with the power delivered by its V6 engine, and it was prone to spinning at the merest provocation.

SUZUKI X90 *(1997–99)*

The X90 was nothing if not brave. With the global car market forever branching out into more and more unusual niches, Suzuki hit on an unexplored market area all of its own when it introduced its new four-wheel-drive model in 1997. The X90 was the world's first—and only—two-seater, sports car off-roader. Or at least that's what it was meant to be.

In truth, it was nothing more than an old and largely unpleasant Vitara, with an underpowered 1.6-liter engine and all of the model's practicality removed to scale down the cabin and replace it with a bubble that looked vaguely like an aircraft cockpit. The X90 was neither fast, sporty, nor sensible as an off-roader; to put it more bluntly, it was useless. Why on earth did they bother?

SPECIFICATIONS	
TOP SPEED:	111mph (179km/h)
0–60MPH (0–96KM/H):	10.5secs
ENGINE TYPE:	in-line four
DISPLACEMENT:	92ci (1590cc)
WEIGHT:	2180lb (981kg)
MILEAGE:	30mpg (9.4l/100km)

Left: *Suzuki tried its best to hide the X90's styling by showing only the tail light on the brochure cover. The true horrors were revealed when you turned the page.*

Was it a 4x4, or a sports coupé? While the roof suggested the latter, the rest of the X90's styling pointed firmly to the car's Suzuki Vitara origins.

Power came from a standard Vitara engine, meaning it wasn't especially quick, nor was it refined or economical. Few buyers were impressed, and the X90 was a giant flop.

The X90 failed to deliver any kind of dynamic thrills. It also had dire ride comfort, with the suspension thumping and crashing over uneven surfaces.

TRIUMPH MAYFLOWER *(1949–53)*

With post-war austerity still hanging over Britain, Standard Triumph recognized a gap in the market for a model that had all the trappings of a luxury car, but which was clothed in a compact body and equipped with a low capacity, economical four-cylinder engine. The Triumph Mayflower could have been a huge success, but Triumph took the traditional styling a little too far, giving it the appearance of a Rolls-Royce Phantom that had been chopped in the middle. The razor-edge upper styling and curved lower panels looked decidedly stupid when mated together and, to make matters worse, the crude chassis made for perilous handling, along with a fairly wayward steering setup and brakes that were little more than a token gesture. The Mayflower was dropped after just four years, even though it had been reasonably popular with middle-class buyers.

SPECIFICATIONS

TOP SPEED:	63mph (101km/h)
0–60MPH (0–96KM/H):	no figure available
ENGINE TYPE:	in-line four
DISPLACEMENT:	76ci (1247cc)
WEIGHT:	2016lb (907kg)
MILEAGE:	39mpg (7.2l/100km)

Left: *Advertising in the UK during the 1950s was always fairly reserved and lowbrow. "Britain's New Light Car" was hardly the snappiest of slogans to draw prospective buyers into the showrooms.*

Under the hood, the Mayflower came with a pre-war side-valve engine, which offered dismal performance. It was also coupled to an unpleasant column-change gearbox.

The Mayflower was designed to look like a miniature Rolls-Royce Silver Dawn, so two-tone paint and a noticeable "waistline" in the body were de rigeur. But it was so small, it just looked pretentious and silly.

Handling was dangerous. The car's simple construction and crude suspension, along with the upright body, meant that it leaned badly in corners and lurched out of control if driven too quickly through a turn.

Glossary

bearings Rollers usually made of steel that facilitate the reduction of friction between moving parts on automobiles, such as wheels, steering, and engine components.

cc The abbreviation for the unit of volume cubic centimeter.

chassis The underlying frame of a car that holds together the axles with the body.

ci The abbreviation for the unit of volume cubic inch.

cylinders The parts of the engine that house the pistons, which transfer energy to the axles from the combustion of fuel.

diesel A type of engine that uses fuel known as diesel.

fiberglass A durable material made from glass in fiberous form.

floorplan The arrangement of the floor in a car, such as where the seats, console, and storage are positioned.

handling A term that refers to how well a car reacts to changes in movement, such as turns, acceleration, and deceleration.

hatchback A type of car with a door as access to the trunk.

km The abbreviation for the unit of length known as the kilometer.

LCD dashboard A dashboard in a car that uses LCD (liquid crystal display) technology to illuminate the console.

metallics Paints that appear to have a metal finish.

motoring A term used primarily in Europe that refers to driving.

mpg An abbreviation for miles per gallon, or the amount of fuel efficiency a car has.

nose The front end of a car.

PVC An abbreviation for the material polyvinyl chloride.

quarter panel The body part of a car that is located at any one of the four corners, either the front left, front right, rear left, or rear right.

tail The back end of a car.

upmarket A term that refers to higher quality or more expensive cars.

V6 An abbreviation that means six valves, referring to the power of the engine.

V8 An abbreviation that means eight valves, referring to the power of the engine.

For More Information

Antique Automobile Club of America

501 W. Governor Road

P.O. Box 417

Hershey, PA 17033

Web site: http://www.aaca.org

(717) 534-1910

The aim of the Antique Automobile Club of America is to preserve the memory of the "pioneer days" of automobiling and to keep in the public consciousness antique cars and their spirit.

Classic Car Club of America

1645 Des Plaines River Road

Des Plaines, IL 60018

Web site: http://www.classiccarclub.org

The Classic Car Club of America prides itself on preserving the world's finest automobiles that were made from 1925 to 1948.

Gilmore Car Museum

6865 Hickory Road

Hickory Corners, MI 49060

(269) 671-5089

Web site: http://www.gilmorecarmuseum.org

The Gilmore Car Museum celebrates cars of old and their place in automotive history.

The Historical Car Club of Pennsylvania

P.O. Box 688

Havertown, PA 19083

Web site: http://www.historicalcarclub.org

The Historical Car Club of Pennsylvania has over 700 members from the eastern United States who are dedicated to the ongoing enjoyment of antique, classic, and modified vehicles.

Nash Car Club of America

1N274 Prairie

Glen Ellyn, IL 60137

Web site: http://www.nashcarclub.org

All members of the Nash Car Club of America receive information about all members and their cars and the *Nash Times*, a bimonthly newsletter.

Society of Automotive Engineers

SAE World Headquarters

400 Commonwealth Drive

For More Information

Warrendale, PA 15096-0001
(724) 776-0790
Web site: http://www.sae.org
The Society of Automotive Engineers provides all sorts of technical information used in designing, building, maintaining, and operating automobiles. The society has more than seventy-five thousand engineers, business executives, educators, and students from around the world.

WEB SITES

Due to the changing nature of Internet links, Rosen Publishing has developed an online list of Web sites related to the subject of this book. This site is updated regularly. Please use this link to access the list:

http://www.rosenlinks.com/wwid/woca

For Further Reading

Adler, Dennis. *The Art of the Automobile: The 100 Greatest Cars*. New York, NY: Collins, 2000.

Chapman, Giles. *Worst Cars Ever Sold*. London, England: Sutton Publishing, 2007.

Cheetham, Craig. *The Encyclopedia of Classic Cars*. New York, NY: Thunder Bay Press, 2003.

Fetherston, David. *Chrysler Concept Cars 1940-1970*. North Branch, MN: CarTech, 2008.

Leuthner, Stuart. *Wheels: A Passion for Collecting Cars*. New York, NY: Harry N. Abrams, 2005.

Newbury, Stephen. *The Car Design Yearbook 6: The Definitive Annual Guide to All New Concept and Production Cars Worldwide*. New York, NY: Merrell, 2007.

Peters, Eric. *Automotive Atrocities: Cars You Love to Hate*. Osceola, WI: Motorbooks, 2004.

Sharf, Frederic. *Future Retro*. Boston, MA: MFA Publications, 2005.

Index

Index